Worship Unprecedented

Kingdom Foundations in Worship

Doneta Dawson

Dedication

The things that I have learned and have been able to pen, teach and sing could not have happened without a close relationship with the Holy Spirit. Though that might seem a bit odd for a dedication I must give acknowledgements where they are due.

From the devotional services, to the transition to Praise and worship teams, I am thankful for the houses of worship that allowed me to use the gift God has given and receive life experiences that birthed this book. True Holiness Church of God, H.O.P.E. Word Church of God, Life Changing Ministries, Loving Life Ministries, The Pharmacy Café, Life Changers International, and Authority of the Believers ministries, United Faith Center ministries international, countless conferences and more.

I want to especially recognize people that were instrumental in my development with their ability to equip in worship. Min. Valerie Green, Elder Tracy Lee, Pastors Aaron and Tracy Mathews, Bishop Jeff and Apostle Dee Davis, Apostle Anita Flagg, Prophet Sheryl Warren-Smith, Pastor Deborah Gaston, Apostles Robert and Dixie Summers, Apostle Brian and Prophet Penny Carroll.

Finally, I would like to thank my family for giving me the space to be Wife, Mama, and minister to so many. My loving silent sniper in the spirit of a husband, Quincy Dawson, and my beautiful children Alexandria Sloan-Harper, and Quincy Sloan-Dawson Jr. We all know that home is the first ministry and it takes a lot to dedicate so much of your time and still be present in your family's life. I have tried my best to keep balance and that is why this book is being published NOW. Thank you I love you and am you all's biggest cheerleader!

Preface

The audience of 'Worship Unprecedented' is Believers of Christ that desire to go deeper in worship and learn about the Kingdom of God.

Those that desire to go beyond typical corporate worship to tap into the presence of God like never before. That desire to go beyond the prevailing method in our charismatic churches of 3 fast songs (warm the crowd up), 2 slow songs (draw them deeper into the intimate songs), Announcements, Offering, Preached word, Altar call, and dismissal. Those that want to see beyond a system that is controlled by racism and division in the body of Christ.

Instead Worship Unprecedented changes the paradigm of the individual believer and spurs one to look deeper into the Gospel of the Kingdom of God (Beyond the cross) and in turn worship, reverence, and build relationship with the King of kings, and the Lord of lords. When the Individual believer's paradigm begins to shift then a change begins to happen, internally. And it is affected externally in everyday life, unlike the Sunday (Service) – Wednesday (Bible Study) –Thursday (Choir Rehearsal) ritual/tradition driven believer.

So if you have picked up this book and you desire to know more, go further in your relationship with God through Worship and devotion, you are on the right path.

Table of Contents

Introduction

The Bible is a book about a King, His Kingdom, and His Children. From Genesis to Revelation the King is establishing his Kingdom through his Children on earth. What does this have to do with worship you ask? EVERYTHING!

As our understanding of God's purpose in the earth is understood, then our purpose begins to make sense as well, as children of God. Praise and Worship is more than just a song on Sunday it is a lifestyle carried out every day of the week. The songs, music, dance, artistry, and corporate gatherings are the results of worship. Through this book we will look at all aspects of Worship, the different models and styles of worship biblically from OT to NT in the bible to those in operation today, and how the Prophetic can enhance worship encounters and is in dire need today. We will explore the gospel of the Kingdom of God which is the only Gospel that Jesus ever preached and why it is so important for us as believers to know the Gospel of The Kingdom of God more than we understand church protocol and how it will heal and change the world through us God's children.

Buckle up in the pages to come because as you will experience a shift in perspective which will change everything…..

Chapter 1: The Kingdom of God

A Kingdom Mindset encourages all saints to be ministers in the marketplace. A church mindset merely trains people to serve in church on Sundays. We can serve the church and enjoy it while our own vision is taking shape.

A kingdom mindset speaks to the rule of God over the entire created order. A church only mindset speaks of the rule of God through deacons and elders over those in a church congregation.

A Kingdom mindset is concerned with extending Kingdom citizenship to its born again converts, a church only mindset is concerned with church membership.

A Kingdom mindset builds the organism of the Ekklesia to further advance and equip born again converts, a church only mindset builds the organization of the business of Church as usual with religious repetitious practices that instill tradition while missing revelation of true transformation that comes through relationship, conversion and Kingdom principles applied.

A kingdom mindset connects the revelation of the bible being a book about a King, His Kingdom, and His Children in every account given from Genesis to revelation and how it affects and equips the Ekklesia.

A church only mindset looks as most of these same accounts as bible stories, fictional at best, to demonstrate learning techniques, and lessons for the traditions of men to make them good people in the next Sunday school lesson, Bible study and Vacation bible school.

A Kingdom mindset creates a narrative of worship that focuses on the King and our

relationship with Him as heirs. A church only mindset creates a narrative of worship that focuses on us, our shortcomings and pleads for a visitation.

Let us explore deeper…

Psalm 145:10-13

[10] All thy works shall praise thee, O LORD; and thy saints shall bless thee.

[11] They shall speak of the glory of thy kingdom and talk of thy power.

[12] To make known to the sons of men his mighty acts, and the glorious majesty of his kingdom.

[13] Thy kingdom is an everlasting kingdom, and thy dominion endureth throughout all generations.

The Kingdom of God is God's divine rule and reign and government and Lordship in relation to the world and His children. The Kingdom Originated in Heaven and extended to the earth in attempts to colonize and commune with his creation in Genesis 1.

Kingdom is one word made up of two parts Kings-Domain

In Greek Kingdom is translated Basileia.

King - male ruler of an independent state, especially one who inherits the position by right of birth
Domain - an area of territory owned or controlled by a ruler or government

According to Strong's Concordance:
Original Word: βασιλεία, ας, ἡ
Part of Speech: Noun, Feminine
Transliteration: basileia
Phonetic Spelling: (bas-il-i'-ah)
Short Definition: kingship, sovereignty, authority, rule, kingdom
Definition: kingship, sovereignty, authority, rule, especially of God, both in the world, and in the hearts of men; hence: kingdom, in the concrete sense.
932 *basileía* (from 935 */basileús*, "king") – properly, *kingdom*; the realm in which a king sovereignly rules. A *kingdom* (932 */basileía*) always requires a *king* – as the kingdom (932 */basileía*) of God does with *King Jesus*! 932 (*basileía*) especially refers to the rule of

Christ in believers' hearts – which is a rule that "one day will be universal on the physical earth in the Millennium" (G. Archer).

[The *kingdom* (<u>932</u> /*basileía*) is constantly used in connection with *the rule of Christ in the hearts of believers* – which also extends in various *stages*.]

Jesus Christ came preaching one Gospel, John the Baptist came preaching one Gospel, the disciples and later Apostles recorded came preaching one Gospel. The Gospel of the Kingdom of God, which is the Gospel (Good News) of Jesus Christ. Somehow over the course of history this has been watered down to many different variations of the cross.

Jesus NEVER proclaimed these variations of the Gospel that is being preached today. The gospel of the Death, Burial, and Resurrection of Jesus Christ is necessary, but it is only PART of the Gospel. There has been severe neglect to mention his Kingship, The Kingdom from which he Reigns and our relation to Him in this light as born again of incorruptible seed to have rule and dominion and subdue in the earth under the created order of God. The reason for the proclamation of the Kingdom of God being near was good news, because of a hope and expectation for God's Kingdom prophesied throughout the scriptures.

I have taught classes for years and in my entire religious walk with God never even thought to understand what the Gospel of the Kingdom of God was. I thought the Kingdom meant "The Church". 'Kingdom meaning Kings Domain, well that must be us, so we are the Kingdom'. This was my thought and philosophy, until the Holy Spirit began to speak and urge me to seek the Kingdom of God. What I found out is that WE are not the Kingdom of God. The Kingdom of God was the focal point in all of Jesus's sermons, and the deliverances, healings and miracles that followed. All throughout the Old Testament they continually talked about this "Kingdom", even in the book of Genesis God hints towards this Kingdom rule extended from heaven to earth. After recapping some of the greatest stories ever told in the bible in the Old Testament, they all dealt with Government and establishing a Kingdom for the Children of God.

Let us look at it from Genesis. We will start at Genesis 1:26 after the earth was created by proclamation of God, he then created us (humankind) and gave a charge to us:

Gen 1:26-28: **26Then God said, "Let us make mankind in our image, in our likeness, so that they may rule over the fish in the sea and the birds in the sky, over the livestock and all the wild animals, and over all the creatures that move along the ground."**
27 So God created mankind in his own image,
in the image of God he created them;
male and female he created them.
28 God blessed them and said to them, "Be fruitful and increase in number; fill the earth and subdue it. Rule over the fish in the sea and the birds in the sky and over every living creature that moves on the ground."

Let me reiterate Genesis 1:1-25 was the creation of

all things by God. It is almost as if he is duplicating or creating a smaller version of his dwelling in heaven on the earth and colonizing or "appropriating (a place or domain) for His own use." It is at this point that he makes an image and likeness of Himself to tend or care for His creation. So, he creates this being then gives it the charge of Fruitfulness, dominion, and rulership.

Rule - one of a set of explicit or understood regulations or principles governing conduct within a activity or sphere.

This would imply that we are given a measure of governing to conduct in our sphere which is the earth. This also places a responsibility upon us to care for the earth and things of earth to preserve it. So, when we see wars, killings, sickness, disease and afflictions we cannot blame God. This was our dominion to keep and because of the deceitfulness of our hearts birthed through sin we have destroyed a lot but we can always rebuild and thanks be unto

God for redemption to cleanse us and give us a new heart through Christ our Lord and Savior and King. Also note that in this passage it says that we are to have rule over all creatures in the sea, sky or any creature that creeps upon the earth. There is one thing that we DO NOT have Dominion over in the earth… Each other! That was for God to do. And as you look throughout the scriptures you will see that this is what God designed for us in the first place.

God called Abram out of a pagan nation to establish his Kingdom, God set Joseph up to preserve His children while in time of famine in a pagan government. God called Moses to deliver his children from the hand of the Egyptian Pharaoh to establish his Kingdom, God called Joshua to take his children into the promised land to establish his rule amongst them and establish His Kingdom. God set up his government of Judges to rule over his children and consult with Him to establish His Kingdom, God although rejected of His own children allowed them to choose their own King that they could see with their eyes and reverence him like the pagan nations around them through King Saul to establish His Kingdom. God then chose King David to take over the throne from King Saul because he knew that David would consult him on all matters in handling the care of His Kingdom, and so on and so forth....

As you read through the Old Testament you will actually begin to see a theme. "The Kingdom". There are more scriptures about Government, rule, opposition, and reckoning then there are items about the temple (Old Testament Church). Why do you think that is?

It is because the Kingdom of God is the number one priority of God. The prophets would proclaim the words and actions of God to the children of Israel and to Kings and Governments to establish his Kingdom Rule in the hearts of his Children. The laws of God constituted the principles of the Kingdom and in an effort to separate the children of Israel from mixing the cultures of the pagan nations around them to the

Culture of the Kingdom that was being established to them.

So there is this journey presented that the children of God are attempting to get to this place where they can establish the Kingdom of God and live in relation to him, but there is also this struggle that comes from the heart of man that is born into him because of the disobedience of his forefather Adam. That struggle is Sin. The word of God says that 'all unrighteousness is sin' according to 1John 5:17 And because of the sin of Adam an entity can enter the hearts of mankind and make it wicked and deceitful. Sin. In the Old Testament the only thing that would redeem a person from sin was atonement. Atonement means - reparation for a wrong or injury or expiation for sin.

This is where the temple or church would come into play. There were a designated people whose lives were dedicated to service unto God and atoning the sins of the children of God. Atonement could only be redeemed by blood sacrifice. The Shedding of Blood would remit the sin of the sinner and put them back in right standing with God. The act of atonement could only be performed by these designated people because they were raised to uphold the laws of the Lord and live a perfect clean and holy life. Those people were the priests. The priests of God were the mediators that atoned on behalf of the children of God. In the Old Testament they took an Oath and dedicated their lives to this service. But there was one small problem. They too would sometimes break the oaths, commit sins and have differing opinions of the laws of God and how to carry them out. The Priests in the Old Testament would then split into sects amongst the Israelite nation and become Pharisees and Sadducees.

So for all of the systems set in place and the issues with the Priesthood keeping their oaths the prevailing disobedience of the children of Israel and the hope for the Kingdom of God to truly be established for His Children, God sent his son to the earth to reconcile the priesthood and bring the Kingdom to His children.

Isaiah the Prophet, Daniel, and many other Prophets Prophecy of the coming of this King that would reign and the government would be upon his shoulder and that he would crush all other kingdoms:

Daniel 2:44 NIV: **"In the time of those kings, the God of heaven will set up a kingdom that will never be destroyed, nor will it be left to another people. It will crush all those kingdoms and bring them to an end, but it will itself endure forever."**
Isaiah 9:6-9 NIV: For to us a child is born, to us a son is given, and the government will be on his shoulders. And he will be called Wonderful Counselor, Mighty God, Everlasting Father, Prince of Peace. Of the greatness of his government and peace there will be no end. He will reign on David's throne and over his kingdom, establishing and upholding it with justice and righteousness from that time on and forever. The zeal of the LORD Almighty will accomplish this.

So these were proclamations and prophecies of this King to come and bring the Kingdom of God with him. Let's fast forward to Jesus and John's entry to the

Children of God after 400 years of Silence to the Children of Israel.

Matt 3:1 - In those days John the Baptist came, preaching in the wilderness of Judea 2 and saying, "Repent, for the kingdom of heaven has come near." 3 This is he who was spoken of through the prophet Isaiah:
"A voice of one calling in the wilderness,
'Prepare the way for the Lord,
make straight paths for him.' "[a]

Matt: 4:17 - From that time on Jesus began to preach, "Repent, for the kingdom of heaven has come near."

From this point going forward Jesus Christ taught, demonstrated, and proclaimed the Kingdom of God to all men. Even through his persecution, death, burial and resurrection he referenced and made plain the Kingdom of God. After reading this chapter if you go back into your bible you will actually begin to discover that the Kingdom of God has been hidden in plain sight.
Jesus then fulfilled the law and the prophets in (Read) Matt 5:17, Mark 9:2-10, Luke 17:1-9

And then released the Kingdom of God to its citizens through the Holy Spirit in Acts 1:1-10, and Acts 2.

Now we have received the Kingdom of God and his Rule and Reign through the promise that spoken in the scriptures listed above the Holy Spirit allows us access to begin to apply the teaching, and demonstration that Jesus Christ instructed in the Gospels up until his Death, Burial and Resurrection.

17 For the kingdom of God is not a matter of eating and drinking, but of righteousness, peace and joy in the Holy Spirit

1 Cor.4.20 For the kingdom of God is not in word, but in power.

Luk.17.20-21 And when he was demanded of the Pharisees, when the kingdom of God should come, he answered them and said, The kingdom of God cometh not with observation.21 Neither shall they say, Lo here! or, lo there! for, behold, the kingdom of God is within you.

As an ambassador of the Kingdom of God it is imperative to know what the Kingdom of God is how we belong to it and the authority that we have as Kingdom Citizens.

One of the greatest things in earth is to understand who you are. Not based on bloodlines, labels, or preconceived notions but by connecting to your creator and allowing Him to reveal it to you. Once you can identify who you are then a lot of the things that hold us back will begin to cease. When you accept Jesus Christ as Lord and Savior you are then born again into the Kingdom of God and you become a Saint of the God. You identify as a saint and son of God then your entire perspective, value, and quality of life and what you were put on earth to do changes and so it reflects in your worship, praise, and your everyday life.

Chapter 1: The Kingdom of God

1. What is the Kingdom of God?

    _____

    _____

    _____

2. Give an example of Kingdom Mindset vs
    Church only Mindset

    _____

    _____

    _____

3. What scripture highlights God's original plan
    to extend the Kingdom of Heaven rule to the
    earth and through whom?

    _____

    _____

    _____

4. What does Atonement Mean?

    _____

    _____

    _____

5. How did God's government operate before the Children desired to function like cultures around them?

_____

_____

_____

_____

6. There is more scripture dealing with the government than the temple in the Old Testament. True or False?

_____

_____

7. Jesus preached, taught and demonstrated the Kingdom of God to his disciples, when did he give it to them and how?

_____

_____

_____

_____

Chapter 2: Worship

"Let him kiss me with the kisses of his mouth-- for your love is more delightful than wine." Song of Solomon 1:2 NIV

You did not give me a kiss, but this woman, from the time I entered, has not stopped kissing my feet. Luke 7:45 NIV

"He has brought me to his banquet hall, and his banner over me is love" Song of Solomon 2:4 NIV

"God is spirit, and his worshipers must worship in the Spirit and in truth." John 4:24 NIV

"Come, let us bow down in worship, let us kneel before the LORD our Maker;" Psalm 95:6 NIV

"I bow down toward your holy temple and give thanks to your name for your steadfast love and your faithfulness, for you have exalted above all things your name and your word." Psalm 138:2 ESV

Ah the great days of leading worship! I remember when I would come in and 'set the atmosphere' for corporate worship. That required fasting and praying, consulting the Lord for a song to sing, preparing my mind heart and soul for service, only to get in the car and make the trek to service yelling at everyone to shut up, arguing or picking at each other, griping with my husband about us being late because we couldn't find the right socks, or someone forgot to eat breakfast, or whatever other distraction presented itself that morning. Wondering who was going to show up late on the team to open service and yep it will be the same person as last time if not me. All the hustle, and bustle to make it to service only to pray with the team have an amazing service and never even think about all the preparation that I had put in that morning. I had the formula down, but there was a lot missing when it came to understanding worship. I thought it was partly my responsibility to set everyone's atmosphere for worship to usher in the presence of God. Only to be frustrated because here I was pumping the people up and nobody really moved. It was when I would shift my focus to God that I would see a change in the people. I later learned that 'setting the atmosphere' was not something to be done for someone else. You see, the atmosphere was not the same as a natural atmosphere of oxygen and the space in a room. No, the atmosphere that I set for any type of worship corporate or personal is in one place, my own mind and heart. What I came to realize is a saying that I would later use when I teach "Attitudes are contagious, is yours worth catching?" Meaning when in a corporate setting there is no need to force anyone to participate, but instead that true worship and praise is contagious. The love displayed toward God will become infectious in a corporate setting because the focus has shifted from people to God! When it comes to understanding that worship is not just for Sunday and midweek services, then and only then will the awareness of 'setting atmospheres', and worshiping God in spirit and in truth take on a completely different meaning. Let us explore worship…

What is Worship? Worship in the bible is translated two ways. The Old Testament is written in Hebrew, and the New Testament is written in Greek so there are two different pronunciations, and meanings but they arrive at the same conclusion. Worship in Greek is the word "Proskueno" it means kiss with adoration (like a dog that licks its masters hand), in Hebrew it is the word "Sagad" or "Shachah" and means to fall down, or to bow down in reverence. Root meaning adore and revere.

Worship is not a slow song, or a fast one for that matter…Worship is not our tears…Worship is not our dancing and expressive shows of love…Those things are the RESULT of worship. Worship is a lifestyle for the believer. Worship is a lifestyle of obedience and devotion. Worship is sacrifice. Worship is the bowing of the heart.

In every culture and in every religion, there is

worship. False gods and even the True and Living God adore worship. Along with dominion and fruitfulness, one of the greatest things about the relationship between man and God is worship, communion, and relationship. Adam and Eve had a relationship with God. Adam would walk and talk to God in the cool of the day. It was sin that broke that place of intimacy with God in the Garden of Eden. Jesus Christ came and fulfilled the law and redeemed us to tear the veil that separated mankind from God so that we could have communion with him again!!

In the Old Testament when Cain and Abel, or Abraham, or Elijah, or Job went to Worship the Lord it consisted of a sacrifice. There was no mention of songs being sung, or dancing, or even instruments for that matter. So how can we limit worship to a song? They all used sacrifices to the Lord. A sacrifice of time, of their economy, a sacrifice of their livestock and they would build an altar to the Lord of wood and burn the sacrifice on that altar. It was only Blood that could redeem or remit the sins of people in worship so there was a lot of that type of sacrifice required and done. They also had to be obedient and intentional about their offerings to the Lord. God required that Abraham Sacrifice his own son! WOW! Abraham was obedient to do it and right before he was to complete his sacrifice a ram showed up in a bush and he was able to instead sacrifice it. God tested his obedience. That was worship.

I always wondered, why blood? Why would an innocent animal have to be slaughtered? Why burn his flesh and pour out the blood? I would pray this: "God why does it have to be blood" and God answered.

Lev17:11 NLT: for the life of the body is in its blood. I have given you the blood on the altar to purify you, making you right with the LORD. It is the blood, given in exchange for a life that makes purification possible.

So, it made sense. A lot of people believe that Cain's offering wasn't accepted because it wasn't the first fruit of his labor to God and Abel's was in Genesis 4:3-4, but according to this passage there was a sacrifice of an animal that was rendered acceptable. With the fat portions of the animal there is also blood for atonement. So, it may very well have been the wrong offering that caused it to not be acceptable.

Offering is a sacrifice to the Lord. Thanks, be unto God that Jesus Christ is our ultimate Atonement for the sins of this world and because he shed his blood for the remission of our sins we no longer have to complete this ritual of killing and shedding blood in our worship and offering. Oh, but we are required to give a sacrifice.

Sacrifice is costly. You must give up something in order to offer it. I believe that sacrifice is a pivotal part of our worship with the Lord. We do not sacrifice bulls and goats and lambs, but we do sacrifice our carnal nature, our selfish desires, our old way of thinking, our allegiance to things that block our relationship with him, our lifestyle.

Romans 12:1-2 NLT: 1 Therefore I urge you, brothers, on account of God's mercy, to offer your bodies as living sacrifices, holy and pleasing to God, which is your spiritual service of worship. 2 Do not be conformed to this world but be transformed by the renewing of your mind. Then you will be able to discern what is the good, pleasing, and perfect will of God.

Not only is worship obedience and offering. Worship is a bowing of the heart. Worship is the object of our desires. Bowing is a form of reverence. It places an extremely high priority on the object that it bows to as Royalty, Highness, Kingship and Lord. Though we may not physically give a bowing motion, our hearts do bow in reverence to that which we highly celebrate, devote ourselves to, and desire. We were created to worship and commune with God. I liken it to having this missing piece in our heart that only

God can fill and created to be connected to our Lord, Adonai, Creator, and Abba. Until we understand that this part of us, we will worship other things in its place. We can worship our careers, cars, sports, children, spouses, loved ones, and phones etc. in the place of God. For this reason alone you can understand how some of the wealthiest and most famous people in the world can have all of the earthly goods they desire, a family and marriage, but still feel empty..there is something missing that only God can fill. Our hearts can bow to other things and other people in an instant if our relationship with God is not intact. Sin separates us from even the consciousness of God while we do as we will. But it is repentance and that everlasting atonement of Jesus Christ that puts us in right relationship with God. It is extremely easy to think about whom or what you worship once you have taken your focus off God. Think about the one thing that you do not think that you could ever live without. Once you know what that thing is be very diligent to make sure that it does not take precedence over your relationship with God.

Worship is devotion. Devotion is intentional communion. Webster's definition of Devotion is love, loyalty, or enthusiasm for a person, activity, or cause. When there is love there is devotion. Intentional communion allows the individual to grow in ways beyond their comprehension in worship. To make an intentional choice to pray, read, obey, sing, dance, devote time to your relationship with God will cause a renewing of the mind, a changing of habits, and a shift in perspective about God himself and you the individual. Embracing and understanding the Kingdom of God will create a passion to understand all there is to understand and even then, new revelation of scriptures will spring forth. The Kingdom of God is a treasure which is hidden in plain sight and once revealed will cause a cosmic shift in the realm of worship. I love how Matthew 13:44 states it:

"The Kingdom of Heaven is like a treasure that a man discovered hidden in a field. In his excitement, he hid it again and sold everything he owned to get enough money to buy the field."

When it comes to worship it's not good enough to just know about worship. There will come a time when worship is needed to pull through hard times, adjust attitudes, replace the hopelessness that life can throw our way, and keep focus on God when everything else is vying for our attention. There Are 3 elements within us that can connect to God in worship and praise to go beyond just knowing about God. Those 3 elements are our makeup Spirit/Soul/and Body. Let us explore.

Understanding the human makeup and how it pertains to worship unprecedented is an exciting piece to explore.

There is a process to God's manifestation through our Worship.

We are 3-part human beings, and this is what makes us special as being made in God's image and after his likeness as it states in Genesis 1:26.

We are 1-part Spirit, 1-part Body, and 1-part Soul.

Spirit – Jeremiah 1:5, Ecclesiastes 12:7

Jeremiah 1:5 "Before I formed you in the womb I knew[a] you,
before you were born I set you apart;
I appointed you as a prophet to the nations."(KJV)

Ecclesiastes 12:7 And the dust returns to the ground It came from, and the spirit returns to God who gave it. (KJV)

Body – Genesis 2:7 Ecclesiastes 3:20

Genesis 2:7 Then the LORD God formed a man[a] from the dust of the ground and breathed into his nostrils the breath of life, and the man became a living being.(kjv)

Ecclesiastes 3:20 All go to the same place; all come from dust, and to dust all return. (KJV)

Soul – Genesis 2:7 KJV, Psalm 84:2, Psalm 103:1-2

Genesis 2:7 KJV And the LORD God formed man of the dust of the ground and breathed into his nostrils the breath of life; and man became a living soul.

Psalm 84:2 My soul longeth, yea, even fainteth for the courts of the LORD: my heart and my flesh crieth out for the living God.

Psalm 103:1-2 Bless the LORD, O my soul: and all that is within me, bless his holy name.

² Bless the LORD, O my soul, and forget not all his benefits:

Spirit

Our Spirit is eternal. It existed before our earthly adventure and will exist at the time of our transition from this life to the next. Our Spirit is the part of us that lives in our dreams, in our heavenly communication to our father (will delve into that later) and has been redeemed to life from a death sentence, and from the Kingdom of darkness into the Kingdom of His marvelous light through our Lord and Savior Jesus Christ.

God seeks that we worship Him in spirit and in truth. Your Spiritual language is that of the unknown tongues. It is speaking in your heavenly language. It is your spiritual connect to God that takes you back to the place of eternity and is not tied to time, place, or mental capacity. It extends beyond those earthly borders to connect directly with Abba. When you speak in your heavenly language you no longer are communicating with your soul, or your body but you are communicating spirit to spirit. Your spirit along with the Holy Spirit.

Jesus Promises us that Holy Spirit who is our advocate will be our guide during the spirit to spirit communication.

John 14:16 And I will ask the Father, and he will give you another advocate to help you and be with you forever—

Romans 8:26: In the same way, the Spirit helps us in our weakness. We do not know what we ought to pray for, but the Spirit himself intercedes for us through wordless groans.

Job 33: 14-15: For God does speak—now one way, now another—

　　though no one perceives it.

[15] In a dream, in a vision of the night,
　　when deep sleep falls on people
　　as they slumber in their beds,

1 Cor 15: 45-49 And so it is written, the first man Adam was made a living soul; the last Adam was made a quickening spirit.

[46] Howbeit that was not first which is spiritual, but that which is natural; and afterward that which is spiritual.

[47] The first man is of the earth, earthy; the second man is the Lord from heaven.

[48] As is the earthy, such are they also that are earthy: and as is the heavenly, such are they also that are heavenly.

[49] And as we have borne the image of the earthy, we shall also bear the image of the heavenly.

1 Col 1:18

[18] And he is the head of the body, the church: who is the beginning, the firstborn from the dead; that in all things he might have the preeminence.

[19] For it pleased the Father that in him should all fulness dwell.

[20] And, having made peace through the blood of his cross, by him to reconcile all things unto himself; by him, I say, whether they be things in earth, or things in heaven.

[21] And you, that were sometime alienated and enemies in your mind by wicked works, yet now hath he reconciled

Body

Our Body is this miraculous creation that was formed of the dust of the ground after the image and likeness of God and breathed into to create our living souls. The Body is a miraculous thing when you think about it. One sperm and one egg creating a living moving functioning organism with billions upon billions of cells with the intelligence to protect itself, grow, stretch, compute, recover, and heal.

There are STILL scientists to this day discovering new things about the human body, and I believe that there are STILL wonderful new discoveries to be found. The brain functions and dictated the movements of the rest of the body transmitting neurons throughout the body for effective decision making and cooperation. The heart beats and pumps blood throughout the body, supplying every joint and ligament with ample blood to circulate and function properly. The muscles created for strength, adaptable to any condition that the body goes through. The skeleton holds everything together and regenerates cells. No matter the test the body can ALWAYS adapt.

No matter what body part is functioning or malfunctioning whether it is due to a bad diet, hereditary diseases, organ failures, stresses, physical abuse, or handicap, the stronger organs in the body will pick up the slack for the weaker organs or vessels to keep it alive and functioning. The Body miraculously will protect itself against any threat or danger. Imagine that?

Example: Your body when infection and disease enter the body it will go into a fever to heat up the body and fight off the infection. Your eyelashes keep dirt out of your eyes. When the body overheats it begins to sweat to cool itself off. When the skin is broken by a cut or a scrape the blood cells will come together and form a scab to cover the open skin until it heals and then it peels or falls off.

Your Body whether big or small, short, or tall, wide or thin is miraculously created as a reflection to God of Himself and his Likeness! WOW what a great realization. Jesus Christ the visible image of God 5 fingers, 5 toes, a torso, legs, arms, 2 ears, two eyes, one nose, one mouth!!!

As stated originally worship is not a song, dance, tears, the raising of hands, etc. BUT!! Our response bodily to worship is so necessary. We were created to worship, to praise as well, which is the outward extremity and the vehicle that guides the worship to its destination and that is TRUTH.

Body worship or Praise is when we dance, the waving of our hands, the use of flags, props, pageantry, clapping, all things that require action from our lips or otherwise. So is Singing, shouting, leaping, playing instruments, and any outward extreme of our worship and reverence to him. It is our praise and adoration of Him.

Psalm 139:14 I praise you because I am fearfully and wonderfully made; your works are wonderful; I know that full well
Genesis 2:7 Then the Lord God formed a man[a] from the dust of the ground and breathed into his nostrils the breath of life, and the man became a living being.
Psalm 149:3 Let them praise his name with dancing and make music to him with timbrel and harp.

Soul

And finally, our Souls. The Soul is the makeup of the Mind, Will and Emotions. Our personality is contained in our souls, our ways, our dispositions, our makeup framed from upbringing and our emotional and rational decision making is all a part of our soul. God breathed into Adam and allowed him to become a living soul.

It is the breath of God that creates the living souls. He breathes the breath of life into an individual

46

created being therefore life is of Him. He is the way the truth and the life so that is how we commune with Him.

Our souls are like sponges from the birth until the death. We as humans must be mindful of the soul because our outlook on life is tied to the 3 ingredients that make up the soul. **Our Mind, Our Will, and Our Emotions**. Depending on the things that the soul has been exposed to over its lifetime the filter with which our mind can and will perceive can be perverted and deceived. It can also be framed out of dysfunction. Because of the fall of Adam in the Garden of Eden, the soul of humanity was removed from the close presence with God and the sin was born that causes the soul to die eternally separate from God.

God has always desired a close relationship and communion with His creation but because of sin it separated the people from his close presence. Though worship was available the access to his throne was limited to those anointed and called into the service of worship as representatives for the people in the nation of Israel. All kinds of laws and precepts were put in place because of the lawlessness of sin that ran amongst the children of Israel. Even with the laws, and the priesthood to go to God on behalf of the people, the iniquity of the people kept them separate from God. It was through Jesus Christ's Ultimate Atonement for not only Israel but all mankind and fulfilling the law and the prophets that the New Covenant was formed. At that point, the throne of God and worship was no longer just a place for the anointed priesthood to meet God, but access has been made available for everyone to come to God.

When we are born again upon confession that Jesus Christ is Lord, King, and Son of the Living God, we confess our sin to God and ask forgiveness, then we repent, and we are saved, translated from the Kingdom of Darkness that was made abundant through sin that separates us from God into the Kingdom of God's marvelous Light. Being born again then of the water (water baptism) and the Spirit (Holy

Spirit Baptism) we are now believers and Sons of God.

God so loved this world that even after the disobedience of Adam and Eve he still wanted to commune with his creation. And when creation failed to reach the mark Jesus Christ came into the world to be the example, to fulfill the law as a perfect man, and fulfill the prophecies of the soon coming King and God with us (Emmanuel) to Israel to gather the children of Israel back to their promise land on Mt. Zion and rule over them forever.

All of this is mentioned here to reveal one thing. **Deliverance**. While our Spirit is immediately translated from the Kingdom of Darkness to the Kingdom of God's Marvelous light, our SOUL (mind, will, and emotions) is still being perfected into the vessel of honor to be used for God's Glory.

The enemy of our soul desires to pervert our perception when it comes to worship. He was once the leader of all worship in heaven. There is a ploy to distract even the most disciplined believer from the presence, principles, and perspective of worship.

There are different tools and tactics that can be used to pervert worship in the soul to an emotional exercise without the true reverence of God. To turn the focus of worship outward for appearance sake instead of from the inside out making the whole man for God's use. Our emotions are necessary and important in understanding being made in the likeness of God. We were created in His image and likeness, so our emotions originated from Him. It is okay to have emotions, but it is important to not allow those emotions to dictate your worship but instead be an accessory to the spirit and truth that you live from.

Chapter 2: Worship

1.What is worship?

_____

_____

2.Give the Hebrew and Greek definitions of the word 'Worship':

_____

_____

_____

_____

3.Why was a blood sacrifice required for offering and atonement?

_____

_____

4.What is our Modern-Day sacrifice when we worship the Lord?

_____

_____

5.Discuss a couple of ways that devotion further develops the lifestyle of Worship:

_____

_____

_____

6.List ways that the Mind/Body/Soul worships God

_____

_____

_____

7.Why is Deliverance necessary for worshipers?

_____

_____

—

Notes:

_____

_____

_____

_____

_____

_____

Chapter 3: Praise

Praise the LORD. How good it is to sing praises to our God, how pleasant and fitting to praise him! Psalm 147:1

1Praise the LORD. Praise God in his sanctuary; praise him in his mighty heavens. 2Praise him for his acts of power; praise him for his surpassing greatness. 3Praise him with the sounding of the trumpet, praise him with the harp and lyre, 4praise him with timbrel and dancing, praise him with the strings and pipe, 5praise him with the clash of cymbals, praise him with resounding cymbals. 6Let everything that has breath praise the LORD. Praise the LORD. Psalm 150 NIV

"Bless the LORD, O my soul! O LORD my God, you are very great! You are clothed with splendor and majesty," Psalm 104:1

"Praise is the vehicle that gets us to the place of Worship" ~unknown

What is praise? A question I ask when teaching the Worship Unprecedented class just to gauge the student's answers. I love the responses I get! They go from clapping to lifting of hands to dancing and those are correct, but the heart of praise is quite simple. Think of it like this: When a teacher praises a student, or when a boss praises the work of an employee what do they do? They complement and encourage the individual with praise. Simply put, that is what praise is. A celebration of accomplishment, and personhood. We were created in the image and the likeness of God meaning not only do we look like him, we ARE like him, and just as we love attention, compliments, encouragement, and to be shown love so does our Father in heaven. I like to say we have egos, but He has the Biggest Ego! The King of all eternity Sovereign, Omnipotent, Omnipresent, Omniscient, Alpha, Omega, and Creator of the universe, and most of all Abba?!?! Who WOULDN'T love to have that said about them?

Praise is a verb, meaning to express warm approval or admiration of. Praise is the outward expression of worship. Not only can we praise God with our lips we can praise him with our gifts, our bodies, our creativity. God gives us these magnificent gifts to praise him with so why not use them for his Glory? I love how James says it:

Every good gift and every perfect gift is from above, coming down from the Father of lights, with whom there is no variation or shadow due to change. James 1:17 ESV

Praise is our outward expression of worship. When we bless the Lord with our mouths we speak his praises, we can also bless the Lord in song, on the instruments, in dance, in pageantry, in painting, poetry, or whatever creative outlet you are gifted to use. In the bible David was an avid Praise and Worshiper. He played instruments, sang, danced before the Lord with all his might, and even the way that he ruled his Kingdom was praiseworthy and makes him one of the greatest earthly Kings to reign listed in history. In the New Testament Worship and Praise is not mentioned as much as it is in the Old Testament, but it is present. Jesus himself spoke of it in Luke 19:40 NIV: I tell you," he replied, "if they keep quiet, the stones will cry out."

In response to the Pharisee's religious outrage of Jesus's disciples rejoicing and praising his triumphant entry into Jerusalem in Luke 19:37 ESV: As he was drawing near—already on the way down the Mount of Olives—the whole multitude of his disciples began to rejoice and praise God with a loud voice for all the mighty works that they had seen,

The Hebrew word for praise is **Yadah**, which means to praise and give thanks. Other Hebrew terms for praise is **Yada** which means to be intimately acquainted, **Towdah** which means to the lifting of your hands in praise, and **Halal** which means all praises and is the root word for Hallelujah Jah meaning God so in essence Hallelujah means "All praises to God".

Praise is the vehicle that brings you to the place of total reverence of God and there are many ways to express praise beyond our lips. There is the lifestyle of worship which includes obedience to God's Word there are also movements that denote praise to God as well. In the Hebrew language there are 7 postures of praise that can be referenced in the bible and we'll explore that, but first we want to understand the purpose and ability of praise and why it is important to understand that it brings you into the perspective and heart of God as well as disciplines our flesh to turn away from the lusts of the world that attempt to entangle us.

Postures of Praise are listed in 7 Hebrew words

1. Yadah – Give Thanks
2. Towdah – praise no matter the circumstance
3. Halal - all praises
4. Barak – kneel in blessing
5. Shabach – to shout, a loud shout
6. Zamar – to pluck strings of an instrument or to sing
7. Tehillah – to sing, to laud (song of hymn or praise)

1. **Yadah** – praise, thank, thanksgiving, cast, throw up hands. Gen 29:35 is the record of this kind of praise. Yada is the root word of Yadah it means to be intimately acquainted with someone, or God to understand or acquire Knowledge; to know to discern (learning to discern Gods heart).

2. **Towdah** – to praise no matter the circumstance. Psalm 50: 23 is a biblical account of this. Offering, lifting your hands in praise begins the breaking in the one doing so. It is a praise that is needed to defeat the oppression of the enemy. Raising the hands is a sign of surrender, signaling the enemy that you are given over to God.

3. **Halal** – all praises. To celebrate clamorously. Praise, boast, celebrate, clamorously foolish, to shine, hence, to make a show, to rave, sing, rage, renown. All these forms of praise and offering in an attitude of delight. To be

bright, splendid, to cause to shine, to give light, to deserve praise, radiance is at the heart.......it is the root word of Hallelujah.

4. **Barak** – means to kneel, to bless God as an act of adoration. Biblical examples would be Psalm 95: 6 O come let us worship and bow down; let us kneel (barak) before the Lord our maker. 1 Chron. 29:20, Psalm 34:1, Job 1:21, Psalm 96:2, Psalm 103:1-2, Psalm 18:46.

5. **Shabach** - means to shout, to address in a loud tone, to command, to triumph. Psalm 47:1 O clap your hands all peoples, shout (shabach) unto God with a voice of triumph. Psalm 145: 4 One generation shall praise (shabach) thy works to another and declare thy mighty acts. Other biblical examples: Psalm 63:1-4, Psalm 117:1, Psalm 35:27, and Psalm 106:47.

6. **Zamar** – Means to pluck the strings of an instrument, to sing, to praise; a musical word which is largely involved with joyful

expressions of music with musical instruments. The appeals to the minstrels because they too can praise the Lord on their instruments. Biblical examples are: Psalm 21:13 Be exalted O Lord, in Thine own strength, so will we sing and praise (Zamar) Thy power. Psalm 57:8-9 Awake my glory; awake harp and lyre, I will awaken the dawn! I will give thanks to You, O Lord, among the peoples; I will sing praises to you among the nations.

7. **Tehillah** - to sing, to laud (song of hymn or praise). Derived from the word halal and means the singing of halal's, to sing or to laud, perceived to involve music, especially hymns of the spirit. Spontaneous worship, singing unto the Lord a new Song. Some call it the song of the bride and bridegroom, prophetic psalm, and vertical worship and a breaking forth in psalm to God. Biblical example: Psalm 149: 1 Praise the LORD. Sing to the LORD a new song, his praise in

the assembly of his faithful people other examples are Psalm 22:3, Psalm 33:1, Isa 61:3

Praise is Cultural in nature; it adapts to the culture of a people that come together. If the culture is Hispanic, you would hear more songs with a salsa, or merengue feel to them. Old English style music is more of a hymnal feel for the culture that likes that type of psalm to the Lord and a more traditional approach. African style praise has more of a drum cadence. Music itself reflects highly upon the preferred taste of that group of people that come together in praise.

Praise puts you into a place of gratefulness and thankfulness. Though praise is cultural, worship is universal. Praise is the vehicle that leads us into worship.

Praise can take on many different physical forms. Like dance, mime, clapping of hands, singing, waving flags, lying before the Lord, kneeling, playing instruments etc. There are art forms of expression that are as well used to praise God such as painting, drawing, sketching, spoken word poetry, rap, creating sculptures and jewelry. There is no limit to how praise can be used to Glorify God and because he is the creator and we are made in His image and likeness just as He creates he gives us the ability to create for His glory.

Chapter 3: Praise

1. What is Praise?

_____

_____

_____

2. What are the 7 Hebrew terms commonly used in reference to postures of praise?

_____

_____

_____

_____

3. Explain how praise is cultural?

_____

_____

_____

_____

4. Name a few outward expressions today that are used as praise

_____

_____

Notes:

_____

_____

_____

Chapter 4: Models of Worship
Priests and prophets

There have been many different styles of Praise and Worship that have intrigued me. I would be fascinated from traveling and taking in different kinds of worship styles and I have always been one to want to find how they biblically fit with today's times.

To understand the pattern of Worship it is good to know the foundation that was created for a disobedient people that pointed them to the cross and Christ's fulfillment of all Actions.

Communion – Offering

Before the fall of Adam worship consisted of fellowship in the Garden of Eden according to Genesis 3. After that, was then given the offering of a sacrifice in honor of the Lord for the remission of sins. In the case of Cain and Abel it is noted that Abel's sacrifice was more acceptable because of the type of sacrifice that was considered acceptable and it was received. Abel gave his first fruits of the sheep in worship to God, but Cain gave the harvest of the fruit of the land to God seemingly as a leftover. That speaks to the acceptable offering and worth and reverence of the worship relationship. Noah gave sacrificial offering to the Lord. Abram who then became Abraham gave offerings unto the High Priest ad King of Salem (Peace) and Lord. Even as the children of Israel was established, they gave offerings in terms of worship.

Levitical Worship

Understanding Worship or Praise or any type of devotion to God, it is considered a job dedicated to the temple of God. In the Old testament when God was establishing his Kingdom among Israel, he gave Moses a blueprint for the temple of God. A place where God could dwell and meet the people. A communion of sorts.

Since the children of Israel had not yet reached the promised land, they were sojourners traveling to their destination. So, until they were to reach their destination there was still requirement of worship and sacrifice and praise to 1. Purify the people of God for service by remitting their sins and purifying them for service and 2. Establishing and advancing the culture of the Kingdom of God.

While they traveled to this promised land that God had given Moses, they were to create a mobile temple. A mobile place where God can dwell among His people and commune with them. Whenever they would stop, they would put it up and when it was time to move again, they would take it down. I was a tent of meeting and that mobile temple was called a Tabernacle. Today we are the tabernacles of God in Bodily form housing the Holy Spirit, as proposed in Romans 12:1. In the Old testament as Israel was being established each son of Jacob/Israel became a tribe/family of Israel. In total there were 12 sons therefore there were 12 tribes of Israel according to Genesis 29-46 and are the root tribes of all Jewish peoples today. 12 is also the number that represents Government. Are you catching the Kingdom connection there?

Here are the 12 tribes of Israel:

Rueben (Gen 29:32) name means The Lord has seen my affliction and bare me a son

Simeon (Gen 29:33) name means The Lord has heard I was hated so he bares me a son

Levi (Gen 29:34) name means my husband will be joined to me because I bare him 3 sons

Judah (Gen 29:35) name means I will praise the Lord

Dan (Gen 30:6) name means God's judgment

Naphtali (Gen 30:8) name means with great wrestlings I have prevailed

Gad (Gen 30:11) name A troop comes

Asher (Gen 30: 13) name Happy am I call me blessed

Issachar (Gen 30:18) name God has given me my hire I have given my maid to my husband

Zebulun (Gen 30:20) name means God has endued me with a good dowry

Joseph (Gen 30:23-24) means God has taken away my reproach

Benjamin (Gen 35:18) name means God Son of my right hand

Of the 12 sons one of the tribes/families was given the assignment of dedicated service to the Lord that was Levi. So his tribe/family was responsible for the care of the tabernacle the furniture and draperies and veils that belonged to the tabernacle and out of this family the Priests – the mediators between God and man rose up – they were to communicate and go to God on behalf of the children of Israel in both the Tabernacle and once they made it to the promised land, the Temple. It is easy to say that all Priests were Levites but not all Levites were priests.

Daily the priesthood would give offerings to the lord for the people and once a year, the priesthood would atone for the sins of all the tribes of Israel. They would appoint a High Priest to go in to meet with the presence of God and ask forgiveness of the sins of everyone. They would take the blood sacrifice of a spotless lamb under one year old and sprinkle the blood of the lamb upon the altar to ask forgiveness of the sins of Israel. The priests were to live a holy life and depending on the condition of their own heart as they stood before God it could mean the difference between life and death. God could kill them because they were unfit for service of going before him in the Holy of Holies. Prime example of that is mentioned in

Leviticus 10:1-3

10 Aaron's sons Nadab and Abihu took their censers, put fire in them and added incense; and they offered unauthorized fire before the LORD**, contrary to his command.** [2] **So fire came out from the presence of the** LORD **and consumed them, and they died before the** LORD**.** [3] **Moses then said to Aaron, "This is what the** LORD **spoke of when he said:**

"'Among those who approach me
   I will be proved holy;
in the sight of all the people
   I will be honored.'"

Aaron remained silent.

All Priests had steps that they had to fulfill just to get into the presence of God to atone for sin. There was a pattern that the priest hood had to follow to enter God's presence.

They would prepare for service and then enter the outer and inner courts of the tabernacle, burn the sacrificial offering after sacrificing the lamb and sprinkling its blood upon the altar, then they would wash in the Brazen Laver a tub made from mirrors, bronze and other precious metals to clean the priests so that they could robe themselves to enter the holy place and the holy of holies in God. After washing there, the High Priest would then be robed and anointed for service to the Lord in the Holy Place.

Once robed with the garments for entering in the priest would then have a rope tied around his waist and on the robe the bottom of the garment had bells on it. This rope and the bells served an incredibly special purpose. You see only the high priest anointed for service unto god could enter the holy place no one else. And because the Lord would meet with him there, there was a possibility that he may die in the presence of the Lord because of a defiled heart, or any other reason. So, the bells jingled as he moved in the Holy place and that was a way of letting the priests know that he was moving around and alive. If for some reason the bells stopped jingling for any extended period, this would signify that he was dead. Because no one except the high priest could enter the presence of God then the only way to remove the high priest from the Holy place is to pull him out by rope tied around his waist (Exodus 28:35).

Holy Place and Holy of Holies

After the robing of the priests was done then the High Priest would enter the Holy Place. In the Holy Place and Holy of Holies there were 5 items.

- Golden Lampstand
- Table of showbread (Unleavened Cakes)
- Altar of Incense
- The Veil
- And the Ark

The Golden Lampstand

The Golden Lampstand lit up the inside of the tent and its design was given to Moses when he was on the Mount 40 days and 40 nights, it is highlighted in Exodus 25: 31-40 Below:

31 "Make a lampstand of pure gold. Hammer out its base and shaft, and make its flowerlike cups, buds and blossoms of one piece with them. 32 Six branches are to extend from the sides of the lampstand—three on one side and three on the other. 33 Three cups shaped like almond flowers with buds and blossoms are to be on one branch, three on the next branch, and the same for all six branches extending from the lampstand. 34 And on the lampstand, there are to be four cups shaped like almond flowers with buds and blossoms. 35 One bud shall be under the first pair of branches extending from the lampstand, a second bud under the second pair, and a third bud under the third pair—six branches in all. 36 The buds and branches shall all be of one piece with the lampstand, hammered out of pure gold.

37 "Then make its seven lamps and set them up on it so that they light the space in front of it. 38 Its wick trimmers and trays are to be of pure gold. 39 A talent[f] of pure gold is to be used for the lampstand and all these accessories.40 See that you make them according to the pattern shown you on the mountain.

Table of Shewbread

The Table of Shewbread has plates and silverware all beaten gold and it held cakes baked with unleavened (no yeast) bread to commemorate the Passover as highlighted in exodus 25: 23-30

23 "Make a table of acacia wood—two cubits long, a cubit wide and a cubit and a half high.[d] 24 Overlay it with pure gold and make a gold molding around it.25 Also make around it a rim a handbreadth[e] wide and put a gold molding on the rim. 26 Make four gold rings for the table and fasten them to the four corners, where the four legs are. 27 The rings are to be close to the rim to hold the poles used in carrying the table. 28 Make the poles of acacia wood, overlay them

with gold and carry the table with them. [29] And make its plates and dishes of pure gold, as well as its pitchers and bowls for the pouring out of offerings. [30] Put the bread of the Presence on this table to be before me at all times.

The Altar of Incense

The Altar of Incense was the last step in the Holy Place that the priests took before entering the Holy of Holies. The Altar of Incenses represents the prayers of the saints ever lit before the presence of God as indicated in Exodus 30:1-7

30 "Make an altar of acacia wood for burning incense. [2] It is to be square, a cubit long and a cubit wide, and two cubits high[a]—its horns of one piece with it. [3] Overlay the top and all the sides and the horns with pure gold and make a gold molding around it. [4] Make two gold rings for the altar below the molding—two on each of the opposite sides—to hold the poles used to carry it. [5] Make the poles of acacia wood and overlay them with gold. [6] Put the altar in front of the curtain that shields the ark of the covenant law—before the atonement covering that is over the tablets of the covenant law—where I will meet with you.

[7] "Aaron must burn fragrant incense on the altar every morning when he tends the lamps. [8] He must burn incense again when he lights the lamps at twilight so incense will burn regularly before the LORD for the generations to come

The Veil

After reaching the Altar of Incense, the next step in the priest's journey was to go beyond the Veil that separates the Holy Place from the Holy of Holies, where God's presence dwelled. The Veil was created with 11 Curtains of different fabric and colors as God gave Moses the instructions to build it highlighted in Exodus 26:30-34

[30] "Set up the tabernacle according to the plan shown you on the mountain.

31 "Make a curtain of blue, purple and scarlet yarn and finely twisted linen, with cherubim woven into it by a skilled worker. 32 Hang it with gold hooks on four posts of acacia wood overlaid with gold and standing on four silver bases.33 Hang the curtain from the clasps and place the ark of the covenant law behind the curtain. The curtain will separate the Holy Place from the Most Holy Place. 34 Put the atonement cover on the ark of the covenant law in the Most Holy Place. 35 Place the table outside the curtain on the north side of the tabernacle and put the lampstand opposite it on the south side.

Ark of Covenant

Once the Priest come beyond the Curtin or Veil, He is then in the Most Holy Place Called the Holy of Holies. This is the place where the presence of God would come in to meet with the High Priest. In this place the Holy of Holies is one article of Furniture, the Ark of Covenant. The Ark of Covenant was a beautifully crafted box intricately designed with a lid. As stated in Exodus 25: 10-22

¹⁰ "Have them make an ark[b] of acacia wood—two and a half cubits long, a cubit and a half wide, and a cubit and a half high.[c] ¹¹ Overlay it with pure gold, both inside and out, and make a gold molding around it. ¹² Cast four gold rings for it and fasten them to its four feet, with two rings on one side and two rings on the other. ¹³ Then make poles of acacia wood and overlay them with gold.¹⁴ Insert the poles into the rings on the sides of the ark to carry it. ¹⁵ The poles are to remain in the rings of this ark; they are not to be removed. ¹⁶ Then put in the ark the tablets of the covenant law, which I will give you.

¹⁷ "Make an atonement cover of pure gold—two and a half cubits long and a cubit and a half wide. ¹⁸ And make two cherubim out of hammered gold at the ends of the cover. ¹⁹ Make one cherub on one end and the second cherub on the other; make the cherubim of one piece with the cover, at the two ends.²⁰ The cherubim are to have their wings spread upward, overshadowing the cover with them. The cherubim are to face each other, looking toward the cover. ²¹ Place the cover on top of the ark and put in the ark the

tablets of the covenant law that I will give you. [22] There, above the cover between the two cherubim that are over the ark of the covenant law, I will meet with you and give you all my commands for the Israelites.

Under the lid of the Ark were 3 items commemorating the miraculous power and salvation of the children of Israel. Notably the rod of Aaron that budded that Moses used to deliver the children of Israel out of bondage and to cross the Red sea into the wilderness , The two tablets that held the 10 Commandment laws given to Moses on the Mount, and a bowl of manna that God provided for the children for food miraculously in the wilderness for 40 years.

The Glory of the Lord hovered over the Holy of Holies at all times that the children were in the wilderness in a cloud by day and a Fire by night to light to guide and lead the children of Israel into their promised land. The nations of Israel travelled solely by the direction of the Glory Cloud. When the Cloud would move, they would move and when the Cloud would settle, they would settle. On the Day of

Atonement when the priests would enter the Holy of Holies the cloud or Fire of the Lord would come down into the Most Holy Place and meet the High Priest to make atonement and ask the forgiveness of the sins of Israel day and night. This is what happened on the Day of Atonement called Yom Kippur today.

To understand the Pattern of old covenant worship and how it points toward the new it is is imperative to have a full understanding of how new covenant worship works.

There were lots of laws and ordinances and procedures tied to Levitical worship and its necessary functions and all steps of Levitical worship point toward the savior and as well as a reflection or blueprint of heavens mandate for the Israelite nation.

Harp and Bowl Worship

Harp and bowl method of worship is a type of worship made popular by the IHOP movement. IHOP stands for International House of Prayer. They adapted a model of

Worship from Revelation 5:8-12 it is a worship style that incorporates intercession and prophetic utterance.

Revelation 5:8-10NIV: **⁸ And when he had taken it, the four living creatures and the twenty-four elders fell before the Lamb. Each one had a harp and they were holding golden bowls full of incense, which are the prayers of God's people. ⁹ And they sang a new song, saying:**

"You are worthy to take the scroll
**   and to open its seals,**
because you were slain,
**   and with your blood you purchased for God**
**   persons from every tribe and language and people and nation.**
¹⁰ You have made them to be a kingdom and priests to serve our God,
**   and they will reign[b] on the earth."**

This style of worship mimic's heaven's worship where the Harp represents the praises of God and the Bowl represents the prayers of the saints or God's people. It is a continual love song and petition of the people to God that goes forth day and night. In most instances of Harp and Bowl worship it is conducted in a space where there is no program to come behind it. It is a beautiful experience that highlights New Covenant worship.

Davidic Worship

Davidic worship is a term that mimic's its influence, King David. King David was a worshiper at heart that loved the Lord with all his heart. He was very gifted in the playing of instruments, song, dance, and creative in the arts.

David was a minstrel with the ability to play in spiritual dimensions according to

1 Sam 16:23 **23 Whenever the spirit from God came on Saul, David would take up his lyre and play. Then relief would come to Saul; he would feel better, and the evil spirit would leave him.**

David was a Psalmist that wrote and sung and exhorted the people to praise God in Songs unto the Lord whether in distress or in rejoicing in victory according to

Psalm 149: Praise the Lord.[a]
Sing to the Lord a new song,
**   his praise in the assembly of his faithful people.**
2 Let Israel rejoice in their Maker;
**   let the people of Zion be glad in their King.**
3 Let them praise his name with dancing
**   and make music to him with timbrel and harp.**
4 For the Lord takes delight in his people;

he crowns the humble with victory.
[5] Let his faithful people rejoice in this honor
and sing for joy on their beds.

David danced mightily before the Lord with all his heart in rejoicing that the Ark of the Lord was back in His Kingdom

2 Sam 6:14: Wearing a linen ephod, David was dancing before the LORD with all his might, [15] while he and all Israel were bringing up the ark of the LORD with shouts and the sound of trumpets.

New Covenant Worship

The last biblical instruction for worship in the New Covenant that I'd like to cover is listed in 1 Cor. 14:26. This is an instruction of how worship services should flow to a new church that had been established in Corinth. It was instruction to continue to instill the Kingdom of God as well as removing the cultural influences of society and different forms of pagan worship in their region.

1Cor 14:26 [26] What then shall we say, brothers and sisters? When you come together, each of you has a hymn, or a word of instruction, a revelation, a tongue or an interpretation. Everything must be done so that the church may be built up.

Priest and Prophets notable in Worship

These are different types of biblical models of worship from Old Testament to New Testament covered in this chapter. One thing that I want to focus on in these models of worship as well is that there have always been Priests and Prophets to be mediators between God and man in biblical models of worship, even with the new covenant models. Lets looks at the biblical priesthoods that conducted the offerings for worship dating back to Genesis.

Melchizedek was the first recorded High Priest of God and King of Salem. Because there is no record of his beginning or ending it is said that he was Christ in the earth. Abraham tithed to him and Jesus Christ is our High Priest today after the order of Melchizedek according to

Hebrews 7:1-3: **This Melchizedek was king of Salem and priest of God Most High. He met Abraham returning from the defeat of the kings and blessed him, [2] and Abraham gave him a tenth of everything. First, the name Melchizedek means "king of righteousness"; then also, "king of Salem" means "king of peace." [3] Without father or mother, without genealogy, without beginning of** days or end of life, resembling the Son of God, he remains a priest forever.

Gen 14: 18-20: [18] Then Melchizedek king of Salem brought out bread and wine. He was priest of God Most High, [19] and he blessed Abram, saying,

"Blessed be Abram by God Most High,

Creator of heaven and earth.

[20] And praise be to God Most High,

who delivered your enemies into your hand."

Then Abram gave him a tenth of everything.

Asaph Prophets Carried the mantle of prophetic worship as singers and musicians skilled in the art of music. They sang prophetically and carried the spirit of prophecy in their worship so strongly that anyone in their presence would begin to prophesy. They set the atmosphere for God to rule and use whomever he chose to speak his word. They were called on by Kings to come in and minister in Song. They were Regal worshipers.

1 Chron 25:1-2: David, together with the commanders of the army, set apart some of the sons of Asaph, Heman and Jeduthun for the ministry of prophesying, accompanied by harps, lyres and cymbals.

84

1 Chron 15:17-22: So the Levites appointed Heman son of Joel; from his relatives, Asaph son of Berekiah; and from their relatives the Merarites, Ethan son of Kushaiah; [18] and with them their relatives next in rank: Zechariah,[b] Jaaziel, Shemiramoth, Jehiel, Unni, Eliab, Benaiah, Maaseiah, Mattithiah, Eliphelehu, Mikneiah, Obed-Edom and Jeiel,[c] the gatekeepers.

[19] The musicians Heman, Asaph and Ethan were to sound the bronze cymbals; [20] Zechariah, Jaaziel,[d] Shemiramoth, Jehiel, Unni, Eliab, Maaseiah and Benaiah were to play the lyres according to *alamoth,*[e] [21] and Mattithiah, Eliphelehu, Mikneiah, Obed-Edom, Jeiel and Azaziah were to play the harps, directing according to *sheminith.*[f] [22] Kenaniah the head Levite was in charge of the singing; that was his responsibility because he was skillful at it.

Ezra 2:41: [41] The musicians: the descendants of Asaph 128

Neh. 12:46 [46] For long ago, in the days of David and Asaph, there had been directors for the musicians and for the songs of praise and thanksgiving to God.

Zadok Priesthood A company of priests that anointed and Guarded Kings of Israel. Zadok was a Seer prophet that kept the sanctuary when the children of Israel strayed.

1 Kings 1:34: [34] There have Zadok the priest and Nathan the prophet anoint him king over Israel. Blow the trumpet and shout, 'Long live King Solomon!'

1 Kings 1:39: [39] Zadok the priest took the horn of oil from the sacred tent and anointed Solomon. Then they sounded the trumpet and all the people shouted, "Long live King Solomon!

Ezekiel 44:15: "'But the Levitical priests, who are descendants of Zadok and who guarded my sanctuary when the Israelites went astray from me, are to come near to minister before me; they are to stand before me to offer sacrifices of fat and blood, declares the Sovereign LORD.

Ezekiel was a prophet that God used to demonstrate in the arts his judgements for Israel. In mime he used Ezekiel powerfully

Ezekiel 12: The word of the LORD came to me: [2] "Son of man, you are living among a rebellious people. They have eyes to see but do not see and ears to hear but do not hear, for they are a rebellious people.

[3] "Therefore, son of man, pack your belongings for exile and in the daytime, as they watch, set out and go from where you are to

another place. Perhaps they will understand, though they are a rebellious people. ⁴ During the daytime, while they watch, bring out your belongings packed for exile. Then in the evening, while they are watching, go out like those who go into exile. ⁵ While they watch, dig through the wall and take your belongings out through it. ⁶ Put them on your shoulder as they are watching and carry them out at dusk. Cover your face so that you cannot see the land, for I have made you a sign to the Israelites."

⁷ So I did as I was commanded. During the day I brought out my things packed for exile. Then in the evening I dug through the wall with my hands. I took my belongings out at dusk, carrying them on my shoulders while they watched.

⁸ In the morning the word of the LORD came to me: ⁹ "Son of man, did not the Israelites, that rebellious people, ask you, 'What are you doing?'

¹⁰ "Say to them, 'This is what the Sovereign LORD says: This prophecy concerns the prince in Jerusalem and all the Israelites who are there.' ¹¹ Say to them, 'I am a sign to you.'

"As I have done, so it will be done to them. They will go into exile as captives.

¹² "The prince among them will put his things on his shoulder at dusk and leave, and a hole will be dug in the wall for him to go through. He will cover his face so that he cannot see the land. ¹³ I will spread my net for him, and he will be caught in my snare; I will bring him to Babylonia, the land of the Chaldeans, but he will not see it, and there he will die. ¹⁴ I will scatter to the winds all those around him—his staff and all his troops—and I will pursue them with drawn sword.

¹⁵ "They will know that I am the LORD, when I disperse them among the nations and scatter them through the countries. ¹⁶ But I will spare a few of them from the sword, famine and plague, so that in the nations where they go, they may acknowledge all their detestable practices. Then they will know that I am the LORD."

¹⁷ The word of the LORD came to me: ¹⁸ "Son of man, tremble as you eat your food, and shudder in fear as you drink your water. ¹⁹ Say to the people of the land: 'This is what the Sovereign LORD says about those living in Jerusalem and in the land of Israel: They will eat their food in anxiety and drink their water in despair, for their land will be stripped of everything in it because of the violence of all who live there. ²⁰ The inhabited towns will be laid waste and the land will be desolate. Then you will know that I am the LORD.'"

There Will Be No Delay

[21] The word of the LORD came to me: [22] "Son of man, what is this proverb you have in the land of Israel: 'The days go by and every vision comes to nothing'? [23] Say to them, 'This is what the Sovereign LORD says: I am going to put an end to this proverb, and they will no longer quote it in Israel.' Say to them, 'The days are near when every vision will be fulfilled. [24] For there will be no more false visions or flattering divinations among the people of Israel. [25] But I the LORD will speak what I will, and it shall be fulfilled without delay. For in your days, you rebellious people, I will fulfill whatever I say, declares the Sovereign LORD.'"

[26] The word of the LORD came to me: [27] "Son of man, the Israelites are saying, 'The vision he sees is for many years from now, and he prophesies about the distant future.'

[28] "Therefore say to them, 'This is what the Sovereign LORD says: None of my words will be delayed any longer; whatever I say will be fulfilled, declares the Sovereign LORD.'"

The ultimate Priest and Prophet Jesus Christ was the High Priest that fulfilled all the offering, the law, the commandments for the priesthood, and the oaths that even they could not keep. He became the ultimate offering atonement and sacrifice for mankind. He fulfilled the pattern for the Levitical priesthood, and He became the furniture and their purpose in the tabernacle. Upon his death the 11layer veil was ripped from top to bottom and removing the veil that would separate us from God our Father Sovereign King and give us full access to the throne whereby we can cry out "Abba, Father!" Jesus came after the order of Melchizedek "King of Righteous" and "King of Salem" (I speculate that Jesus Christ WAS Melchizedek by their similarities).

Hebrews 7:11-28: [11] **If perfection could have been attained through the Levitical priesthood—and indeed the law given to the people established that priesthood—why was there still need for another priest to come, one in the order of Melchizedek, not in the order of Aaron?** [12] **For when the priesthood is changed, the law must be changed also.** [13] **He of whom these things are said belonged to a different tribe, and no one from that tribe has ever served at the altar.** [14] **For it is clear that our Lord descended from Judah, and in regard to that tribe Moses said nothing about priests.** [15] **And what we have said is even more clear if another priest like Melchizedek appears,** [16] **one who has become a priest not on the basis of a**

regulation as to his ancestry but on the basis of the power of an indestructible life. [17] For it is declared:

"You are a priest forever,

in the order of Melchizedek."[a]

[18] The former regulation is set aside because it was weak and useless [19] (for the law made nothing perfect), and a better hope is introduced, by which we draw near to God.

[20] And it was not without an oath! Others became priests without any oath, [21] but he became a priest with an oath when God said to him:

"The Lord has sworn

and will not change his mind:

'You are a priest forever.'"[b]

[22] Because of this oath, Jesus has become the guarantor of a better covenant.

[23] Now there have been many of those priests, since death prevented them from continuing in office; [24] but because Jesus lives forever, he has a permanent priesthood. [25] Therefore he is able to save completely[c] those who come to God through him, because he always lives to intercede for them.

[26] Such a high priest truly meets our need—one who is holy, blameless, pure, set apart from sinners, exalted above the heavens. [27] Unlike the other high priests, he does not need to offer sacrifices day after day, first for his own sins, and then for the sins of the people. He sacrificed for their sins once for all when he offered himself. [28] For the law appoints as high priests' men in all their weakness; but the oath, which came after the law, appointed the Son, who has been made perfect forever.

The last and final group of Priests were made after the order of Jesus Christ our High Priest that sites at the right hand of the throne today that is the saints. We are kings and priests after the order of Jesus Christ.

Revelation 5:10 [10] And hast made us unto our God kings and priests: and we shall reign on the earth.

1 Peter 2:9: But you are a chosen people, a royal priesthood, a holy nation, God's special possession, that you may declare the praises of him who called you out of darkness into his wonderful light.

Romans 12: 1 Therefore, I urge you, brothers and sisters, in view of God's mercy, to offer your bodies as a living sacrifice, holy and pleasing to God—this is your true and proper worship

Chapter 4: Models of Worship Priests and prophets

1.Name 3 Models of Worship that are prevalent today

_____
_____
_____

2. List the names of the 12 Tribes of Israel

_____
_____
_____

3.Name 3 articles of furniture in the tabernacle

_____
_____
_____

4. List a couple of the Priests and Prophets that were used in worship

_____
_____

5. Jesus Christ forged a better covenant than the priests and prophets of old explain how

_____
_____
_____

6. Since we are king and priest after the order of Jesus Christ how should this affect our worship?

_____

_____

_____

_____

Chapter 5: New Covenant and prophecy

Covenant – Contract or Agreement

Hebrews 7: 11-22 :[11] **If perfection could have been attained through the Levitical priesthood—and indeed the law given to the people established that priesthood—why was there still need for another priest to come, one in the order of Melchizedek, not in the order of Aaron?** [12] **For when the priesthood is changed, the law must be changed also.** [13] **He of whom these things are said belonged to a different tribe, and no one from that tribe has ever served at the altar.** [14] **For it is clear that our Lord descended from Judah, and in regard to that tribe Moses said nothing about priests.** [15] **And what we have said is even more clear if another priest like Melchizedek appears,** [16] **one who has become a priest not on the basis of a regulation as to his ancestry but on the basis of the power of an indestructible life.**

[17] **For it is declared: "You are a priest forever,**
   in the order of Melchizedek."[a]

[18] The former regulation is set aside because it was weak and useless [19] (for the law made nothing perfect), and a better hope is introduced, by which we draw near to God.

[20] And it was not without an oath! Others became priests without any oath,[21] but he became a priest with an oath when God said to him:

"The Lord has sworn
    and will not change his mind:
    'You are a priest forever.'"[b]

[22] Because of this oath, Jesus has become the guarantor of a better covenant.

The old covenant of the nation of Israel consisted of Levitical worship, laws, and the prophets prophesying of this Kingdom and better covenant. There were the Atonements of the people for remission or forgiveness of sins, and the prophets being the mouthpiece for God as the Holy Spirit moved upon them, to establish government, legislature, and to reveal the mind of God to the people. There were also memorials to former miraculous moves of God to keep as a memorial and understanding for how the Jewish faith was come about. All the prophets of God prophesied the new covenant and the future of the Children of Israel. They spoke to the Kingdom rule of God.

Joel prophesied of the ending of the old covenant and the rising of the new covenant and he spoke of a time that the Holy Spirit would no longer move upon set men of God but that He would be upon all flesh and your old men would dream dreams and your sons and daughters would prophesy, that his spirit would be upon all servants, both men and women, he would show wonders in heaven, and on earth(signs and wonders that Jesus did), the sun would be turned to darkness (Crucifixion this happened), and everyone who calls on the name of the Lord would be saved, and that deliverance would go forth. There are some that use this prophecy to dictate the last days now, but this was a prophecy for the end of the old covenant and the birthing of the new covenant.

Daniel Prophesied that at the end of the old covenant that God would set up a kingdom that will never be destroyed, nor will it be left to another people. It will crush all other kingdoms and bring them to an end, but itself will endure forever. Daniel 2:44

Elisha was a representative of the Prophets of Israel and Moses was a representative of the Law of Israel birthed in Mt Sinai when he received the 10 commandments, the Pentateuch, and the blueprint for the tabernacle and Levitical priesthood.

Jesus fulfilled the prophets and the Law of Israel and extended the new covenant promise of entering the Kingdom of God through being born again of the water (baptism and spirit) to have access to all that the new covenant allotted.

In the Gospels Jesus tells his disciples that he is not come to do away with the Law but to fulfill it. That is what grace does. It takes the place of your sin and gives you a second chance to get it right. And so, because the old covenant was based on the Law and the Prophets there is an amazing event that happens to seal the new covenant promise in the gospels about this. Let us read and break it apart this account is found in Matthew 17:

The Transfiguration

Matthew 17: After six days Jesus took with him Peter, James and John the brother of James, and led them up a high mountain by themselves. ² There he was transfigured before them. His face shone like the sun, and his clothes became as white as the light. ³ Just then there appeared before them Moses and Elijah, talking with Jesus.

⁴ Peter said to Jesus, "Lord, it is good for us to be here. If you wish, I will put up three shelters—one for you, one for Moses and one for Elijah."

⁵ While he was still speaking, a bright cloud covered them, and a voice from the cloud said, "This is my Son, whom I love; with him I am well pleased. Listen to him!"

⁶ When the disciples heard this, they fell facedown to the ground, terrified. ⁷ But Jesus came and touched them. "Get up," he said. "Don't be afraid." ⁸ When they looked up, they saw no one except Jesus.

⁹ As they were coming down the mountain, Jesus instructed them, "Don't tell anyone what you have seen, until the Son of Man has been raised from the dead."

10 The disciples asked him, "Why then do the teachers of the law say that Elijah must come first?"

11 Jesus replied, "To be sure, Elijah comes and will restore all things. **12** But I tell you, Elijah has already come, and they did not recognize him, but have done to him everything they wished. In the same way the Son of Man is going to suffer at their hands." **13** Then the disciples understood that he was talking to them about John the Baptist.

Let us dissect this…. You know when I would read this passage of scripture in times past, I always focused only on the fact that Jesus revealed his true self to the disciples by transforming to light. It was not until revelation came forth that I UTTERLY understood the meaning and the importance of this passage. This text is called the transfiguration. Transfiguration means a complete change of form or appearance into a more beautiful or spiritual state. So yes, understanding that he revealed himself is awesome upon reading this passage but there is something a little further that needs to be understood.

Jesus took 3 of his closest disciples upon the mount with him to witness a miraculous transition. Upon coming up the mount they saw Jesus Christ then they saw 3 people. Jesus, Moses, and Elijah…Moses was a representation of the LAW of Israel, Elijah was a representation of the Prophets of Old. There was a transition that took place. While the disciples were astounded and amazed, they were also inundated with old covenant perspective. The first thing that they wanted to do was make a memorial to the 3 by building 3 tabernacles. One for each great man of God, but there was no need. God did not show them the 3 to make a memorial but to witness a transition, a change into a more beautiful or spiritual state….from the Old Covenant (Law and Prophets) being fulfilled into the New Covenant personified (Jesus Christ fulfilling both) and changing his garment and robing to complete fulfillment that would birth this new covenant of Kingdom fulfilled!!!!! He was passing the torch from the Law and Prophets to His dear Son Jesus Christ the FULFILLMENT and ultimate mediator between man and God. How awesome is that?!?!?

After this happened Jesus sworn them to secrecy until his death burial and resurrection, because then it would all be "Finished". And even pointed out how John the Baptist fulfilled the beginning of the end time prophecies that were eluded to in the scripts of old.

There is something that is key to understanding this entire movement that happens during the transfiguration. The disciples because they did not understand what was happening began to revert to their old covenant mindset to build a memorial in the form of 3 tabernacles for Jesus, Moses, and Elijah. But God was not looking for a memorial. He wanted them to WITNESS the transition. I believe that when it comes to our worship, we have a tendency to focus on the mindset of memorializing the presence of God and reverting to the old foundation, when God is beckoning us to transition to what new covenant worship looks like.

Jesus Christ's Birth, Life, Death, Burial and Resurrection gave birth to the prophecies fulfilled and of the prophets of old and the fulfillment of Levitical Laws.

Jesus came to bring a Kingdom to the children of Israel and not only them but the whole world. He never came to bring another religion. While in his time on earth and during his earthly ministry in the Gospels of Matthew, Mark, Luke, and John, He constantly taught about the Kingdom of God in parables, demonstrated the Kingdom and power of God with miracles signs and wonders, and gave an earthly example of living a life of faith.

Amazingly enough, the new covenant did not start with the Gospels. The Gospels merely give preface to the new covenant and the beginning of it. As a matter of fact, in the Gospels Jesus Christ did all the works before sealing the new covenant throughout the Gospels and birthed the Kingdom Age through his Death Burial and Resurrection.

If Jesus did away with the Levitical system of worship and gave the pattern by which we live and dedicate ourselves to God through what we call the Lord's Prayer Matt 6:9-13, why would we to this day continue to conjure up the pattern that has been fulfilled by Jesus Christ himself? Why do we identify ourselves as Levites when in Hebrews

7 it states that not even Jesus Christ identified with the children of Levi and the Levitical priesthood because they could not uphold their vows to live Holy? Jesus came after the order of Melchizedek, out of the tribe of Judah and if we identify with Jesus Christ then our worship should be identified as well in that same vein.

Let us look at how Jesus Fulfilled the broken pattern of Levitical worship.

- In the Levitical Worship Pattern, you had to enter the Outer and Inner Courts. Jesus Stated in John 14:16 I am the way, the truth, and the life: no man cometh unto the Father, but by me. (this makes him the new outer and inner courts)
- In Levitical Worship the priest was required to sacrifice the blood of Lambs and sprinkle the blood upon the altar. Jesus Christ was the ultimate Atoning sacrifice and was quoted as being the Lamb of God slain before the foundation of the world. And because of the blood of this perfect lamb of God we are overcomers Rev 12:11

- In Levitical Worship they would wash in the basin to cleanse them self from the blood naturally and today we wash by the water of the Word (who is Jesus Christ) Ephesians 5:26
- In Levitical Worship they would go into the Holy Place and partake of three things the Lampstand, the Table of Shewbread and the altar of incense. Jesus fulfilled the purpose of all three of these items.
- Jesus Christ is the Light of the World, so he completes the purpose of the lampstand John 8:12Jesus Christ is the bread of life John 6:35
- And the Altar of Incense was a shadow if the intercession of the children of Israel. Jesus Christ sits at the right hand of the throne of God interceding for the saints Rom 8:34
- And he rent (tore) the Veil (Curtain of separation) in two to give us bold access to the throne of grace Matt 17:51, Hebrews 4:16
- There were only 2 laws that Jesus emphasized that we keep today, and they sum up all the commandments in Matthew 22:36-40

[36] "Teacher, which is the greatest commandment in the Law?"

37 Jesus replied: "'Love the Lord your God with all your heart and with all your soul and with all your mind.'[a] 38 This is the first and greatest commandment.39 And the second is like it: 'Love your neighbor as yourself.'[b] 40 All the Law and the Prophets hang on these two commandments."

So, as we seen Jesus has fulfilled the Law, the Prophets, and the mandates for Levitical worship. God is no longer afar off where we have to invite him into our worship, the judgment of the world was placed upon Jesus Christ during the death, burial and resurrection of Christ and so we are no longer in a place of being judged as we would have in the old covenant. We do not have to accept sickness or expect Jesus to come off the throne to 'fix' any issues in our lives. Everything the Jesus ever needed to do for us has been fulfilled and finished and because we have the precious gift of the Holy Spirit promised to us through Joel 2:28, and Acts 1:8, we now have bold access to the throne and we have been given access BACK to the tree of Life, and we have power to 'fix' it ourselves.

Chapter 5: New Covenant and Prophecy Fulfilled

1.What does Covenant mean?

_____

_____

_____

2. The Culmination of the Old Covenant was based on two very important principles the
_____ and the

_____

3. Who represented the Law?

_____

_____

4. Who represented the Prophets?

_____

_____

5. Who is our helper in navigating, understanding, and demonstrating the power of God in the new covenant?

_____

_____

6.As God beckons us to understand new covenant worship what is the ONE thing that we do not want to do that Jesus's Disciples wanted to do when they witnessed the transfiguration?

_____

_____

_____

Notes:

_____

_____

_____

_____

_____

Chapter 6: Holy Spirit and Prophetic Worship

[16] And I will ask the Father, and he will give you another advocate to help you and be with you forever— John 14:16 NIV

Anyone who speaks a word against the Son of Man will be forgiven, but anyone who speaks against the Holy Spirit will not be forgiven, either in this age or in the age to come. Matt 12:32

Peter replied, "Repent and be baptized, every one of you, in the name of Jesus Christ for the forgiveness of your sins. And you will receive the gift of the Holy Spirit. Acts 2:38

Comforter, Teacher, Guide, Gentleman, the Ruach Kadesh of God. Holy Spirit is the living breathing, moving, spirit of God that lives on the inside of born-again believers. He is our Spirit to spirit connection with God. He is our witness of the prophecy which is the testimony of Jesus Christ. He is the gift giver for the Glory of God. He is the 3rd person of the Godhead.

He is a He and not it. You cannot catch him and or lay Him down. He is our connection to the Kingdom, our joy righteousness and peace. He desires to baptize us to overflowing in his spirit so that we can manifest His power to the hopeless and the nonbeliever. He is the revelation of Grace and Mercy that has given us bold access to the throne of God. He is who gives us prophetic utterances and our reminder that God still speaks.

He hovered over the face of the deep when it was void and without form in the beginning of recorded utterances from God in Genesis 1:1. He is the conception with the virgin Mary that birthed Jesus Christ in human form. And he is the comforter given to live in the disciples of Jesus Christ to make saints and witnesses that would extent the rule of the Sovereign King of all kings. He is the Governor of the Kingdom of God that gives daily instruction to the believers.

When we look at Prophecy. The spirit of Prophecy is the testimony of Jesus Christ according to Rev 19:10.

So if there is no bearing witness that Jesus Christ is the Son of God the King of Kings and Lord of Lords then there is no spirit of prophecy but rather divination or heresy.

When it comes to the Prophetic there are prophetic people, and there are Prophets. Prophetic People are highlighted in Joel 2:28 and Acts 2:17

And it shall come to pass afterward, that I will pour out my spirit upon all flesh; and your sons and your daughters shall prophesy, your old men shall dream dreams, your young men shall see visions: Joel 2:28

And it shall come to pass in the last days, saith God, I will pour out of my Spirit upon all flesh: and your sons and your daughters shall prophesy, and your young men shall see visions, and your old men shall dream dreams: Acts 2:17

In the Old Covenant/Testament the holy Spirit would move upon certain men and women as God gave utterance. Usually to the priests and prophets. But the prophecy from Joel was fulfilled in the book of Acts sealing the New Covenant. The Holy Spirit no longer moved upon designated officials, but the Holy Spirit now lives inside the believer upon confession and conversion. The Holy spirit along with living in the believer has other attributes that are worth desiring his presence in the saints. He has gifts that he gives to the believers as well highlighted in 1 Cor 12

1 Cor 12:1 Now concerning spiritual gifts, brethren, I would not have you ignorant.

2 Ye know that ye were Gentiles, carried away unto these dumb idols, even as ye were led.

3 Wherefore I give you to understand, that no man speaking by the Spirit of God calleth Jesus accursed: and that no man can say that Jesus is the Lord, but by the Holy Ghost.

4 Now there are diversities of gifts, but the same Spirit.

5 And there are differences of administrations, but the same Lord.

6 And there are diversities of operations, but it is the same God which worketh all in all.

7 But the manifestation of the Spirit is given to every man to profit withal.

8 For to one is given by the Spirit the word of wisdom, to another the word of knowledge by the same Spirit.

9 To another faith by the same Spirit; to another the gifts of healing by the same Spirit.

[10] To another the working of miracles; to another prophecy; to another discerning of spirits; to another divers' kinds of tongues; to another the interpretation of tongues:

[11] But all these worketh that one and the selfsame Spirit, dividing to every man severally as he will.

[12] For as the body is one, and hath many members, and all the members of that one body, being many, are one body: so also, is Christ.

[13] For by one Spirit are we all baptized into one body, whether we be Jews or Gentiles, whether we be bond or free; and have been all made to drink into one Spirit.

Holy Spirit is special, and he is our connection to God. He is the Key to the Kingdom. There would be no such thing as a prophetic anything with out Holy Spirit.

There are evidences of the Holy Spirit being active in the life of the believer. Some of those evidences are a change in countenance, speaking in other tongues, Speaking in unknown tongues, but most importantly a changed life. A changed life is the best evidence to have of the Holy Spirit being active in our lives. There are a lot of believers that do not speak in tongues for one reason or another. This in no way shape or form disqualifies you from being a saint or saved. You receive a portion of God's spirit when you invite Jesus into your life. Speaking in tongues happens after the baptism or Full Immersion of the Holy Spirit in your life. To receive this gift in past times I have been reminded of religious tarry(wait) services as a child. Tarrying for the Holy ghost in the religious culture was dependent on calling out the name of Jesus repeatedly until you received the baptism of the Holy Spirit and began speaking in tongues. My young mind could never make sense of this but as an adult it made sense. I was asking the Lord to come into my heart and baptize me in his love and spirit. The terminology was different but the sentiment the same. And what I learned is that it does not have to be a tarry service unless that is what you believe it will take for you to receive it. I received it because I invited Holy Spirit in to speak through me with joy and desire. Many others that I know as well did the same. This enables spirit to spirit communication that bypasses human language to heavenly language with Abba.

Holy spirit is a huge part of prophetic worship. As I stated you have prophetic people (every believer should be a prophetic person), where the spirit of God is alive and able to reveal prophetic truths through the believer whenever sought. Then there are Prophets. Prophets do not have a gift but rather they ARE the gift because of the office they hold in the body of Christ. According to Ephesians 4:11-15

Eph. 4:11-15: And he gave some, apostles; and some, prophets; and some, evangelists; and some, pastors and teachers.

[12] For the perfecting of the saints, for the work of the ministry, for the edifying of the body of Christ:

[13] Till we all come in the unity of the faith, and of the knowledge of the Son of God, unto a perfect man, unto the measure of the stature of the fulness of Christ:

[14] That we henceforth be no more children, tossed to and fro, and carried about with every wind of doctrine, by the sleight of men, and cunning craftiness, whereby they lie in wait to deceive.

[15] But speaking the truth in love, may grow up into him in all things, which is the head, even Christ:

Prophets are a Gift of Jesus Christ given to the Body of Christ as one of the 5-Fold offices given to equip the Body of Christ and mature her so that we will not be deceived by the enemy.

Prophets carry the spirit of prophecy because they are the gift to the body as opposed to asking for the gift. They can prophesy with no prompting because they are wired to prophesy. Most that hold the Office of Prophets have prophesied or known things before they happened before ever coming into the knowledge of who they are in Christ. Those that walk in the office of the Prophet are born with the ability. As a matter of fact, most Psychics are confused prophets. They consult another source to receive revelations and they tap into tap into demonic dimensions knowingly or unknowingly and consult with familiar spirits. Just as worship is an important part of the Believers walk that the enemy wants to pervert. He desires to pervert prophecy.

When prophets worship it opens prophetic people to more easily prophesy. Just as the Asaph Prophets mentioned in

Chapter 3 carried the spirit of Prophesy and when they would meet others in their presence would begin to prophesy. It is the same with worshiping prophets today. They carry an atmosphere of Prophecy and release songs of the Bride to the Bridegroom of our souls and Holy Spirit orchestrates it all.

Prophetic activations are exercises that are done with equipping believers that we do actively in our Worship Unprecedented to unlock faith to be used by God and to receive the blessings of the Lord. There are also exercises that Worship teams can do to strengthen the faith and increase hearing the Holy Spirit as we minister to others. It is important to understand that God still speaks and that he loves to commune with us through worship so why prophetic Worship. Below are highlighted the purpose for Prophecy in the new covenant believers in 1 Cor 14:3

[3] But he that prophesies' speaketh unto men to edification, and exhortation, and comfort.   1 Cor 14:3

Chapter 6: Holy Spirit and Prophetic Worship

1.Name a few attributes of Holy Spirit

_____

_____

_____

_____

2. What is the spirit of prophecy?

_____

_____

_____

3.Name some evidences of the Holy Spirit in the life of a believer

_____

_____

_____

4. What is the difference between prophetic people and Prophets?

_____

_____

_____

_____

_____

_____

_____

_____

_____

5. What ability does today's Worshiping Prophets have that is identical to Asaph Prophets?

_____

_____

_____

_____

_____

_____

_____

Chapter 7: The New

So, what does New Covenant Kingdom Worship Look like?

I have had many sessions with mentees and after explaining everything that I have gone through in this book, the question above is the look that I receive. It seems once everything that you have been taught and become familiar with changes, you go through a range of emotions. Feeling lost, deceived, angered, processing, and then finally open to God's process.

Going through this process frees you up to be the worshiper in whom Jesus Christ explains that God is looking for in John 4:23-24
²³ Yet a time is coming and has now come when the true worshipers will worship the Father in the Spirit and in truth, for they are the kind of worshipers the Father seeks. ²⁴ God is spirit, and his worshipers must worship in the Spirit and in truth."

The perception of how to approach God changes. With the entrance of having Emmanuel (God with us) dwelling in the heart of the born-again worshiper, the sentiments change from asking God to search our hearts and cast me not away, to having the promises of the Lord that he will never leave us nor forsake us. We have the ability of our own accord to present ourselves Holy and Acceptable for service unto the Lord because he no longer dwells in tabernacles made with man's hands, but we have become the living moving breathing tabernacles of the Lord. According to 1 Cor 3:16 and Romans 12:

12 Therefore, I urge you, brothers and sisters, in view of God's mercy, to offer your bodies as a living sacrifice, holy and pleasing to God—this is your true and proper worship. ² Do not conform to the pattern of this world but be transformed by the renewing of your mind. Then you will be able to test and approve what God's will is—his good, pleasing and perfect will.

If you stay in Romans 12:3-7 more is revealed about new covenant worship here:

³ For by the grace given me I say to every one of you: Do not think of yourself more highly than you ought, but rather think of yourself with sober judgment, in accordance with the faith God has distributed to each of you. ⁴ For just as each of us has one body with many members, and these members do not all have the same function, ⁵ so In Christ we, though many, form one body, and each member belongs to all the

others. [6] We have different gifts, according to the grace given to each of us. If your gift is prophesying, then prophesy in accordance with your[a] faith; [7] if it is serving, then serve; if it is teaching, then teach; [8] if it is to encourage, then give encouragement; if it is giving, then give generously; if it is to lead,[b] do it diligently; if it is to show mercy, do it cheerfully.

When it comes to the fulfillment of old covenant methods the foundation of the Kingdom of God goes back to our purpose as children of God and Jesus Christ allows us access back to the place in Eden where the tree of life exists. He becomes the tree of Life and our worship is then taken back to the place of Relationship, Reverence, and Worth. That God's original intent of extending his Kingdom toward his creation to be Fruitful, Multiply, Subdue, and Have dominion is now more easily accomplished.

All Kingdoms worship the King. We have been made a nation of Kings and Priests because of Jesus Christ according to Rev 5:10. Because we are a nation of King-Priests the Lord Jesus Christ is King of Kings and Lord of Lords and we bow our hearts in worship to Him.

There is a misconception about the Glory of the Lord being afar off, but that is old covenant perception, referenced when only Moses could enter the presence of the Lord then he had to where a veil to cover his face because the Glory of the Lord was upon him. In the New Covenant worship model, we are Glory Carriers according to 2 Tim 2:21 so that God can be exalted in all the earth. We must humble ourselves to carry his presence with all diligence. Everything that we do and exhibit as Kingdom Ambassadors and believers is to draw people to the Glory of the Lord and not ourselves.

Through Christ the Holy Spirit that lives in you, you have the full Godhead living in you to be able to carry this precious gift:

2 Colossians 2:9-12
[9] For in Christ all the fullness of the Deity lives in bodily form, [10] and in Christ you have been brought to fullness. He is the head over every power and authority. [11] In him you were also circumcised with a circumcision not performed by human hands. Your whole self ruled by the flesh[b] was put off when you were circumcised by[c] Christ, [12] having been buried with him in baptism, in which you were also raised with him through your faith in the working of God, who raised him from the dead.

With these promises being made, we now have freedom to worship God, without wrath or doubting. Isn't that amazing? Holy Spirit is the leader, guide, teacher, comforter, and giver of Gifts. And one of the GREATEST gifts that Holy Spirit gives is that of the ability to prophesy.

Prophesy is communicating the will, heart, and mind of God towards his creation for the edification, exhorting, comfort and perfecting of the saints of God. In the New testament because we all have access to the gift of God that is Holy Spirit we have access to prophecy, and if we pray for the gift Holy Spirit who dispenses the gifts severally as he will can give you that gift. In the old testament the prophets were the only ones that could prophesy. If a man or woman of God of status prophesied, it was because they were amid prophets and the spirit of prophecy was prevailing in that atmosphere.

God loves to communicate with his creation through prophesy, and the sons of God love to know and be reassured that God is with them and hears them and reveals for exhortation, comfort, or edification on many things. To us, Prophecy is much more than just contained in the spoken word there are many different classifications of how Prophecy is used in worship, prayer, writing, in the arts. Minstrels can play the heart of God and stir up the atmosphere for worship, psalmists can sing the words that God wants to convey, dancers can dance the Word of God in movement to communicate what God wants us to see, and artists can use different extremities to communicate the will of God in worship.

We have what we call songs of the Bride (ekklesia- church) to the Bridegroom (God), and Songs of the Bridegroom to the Bride called Vertical Worship.

We are a prophetic people as saints of God by nature of Christ and being made alive in the image of Him and Holy Spirit dwelling in us. But because we have this ability does NOT make us PROPHETS. New Covenant Prophets are called to the Governing Office of the Prophet in the body of Christ and go through a rigorous process of maturity and an apprenticeship to be able to handle the office and all that it entails. It is possible to have Worshiping Prophets as a matter of fact all Prophets worship but not all worshipers are Prophets.

According to the Apostle Paul there was an order set for worship that the church in Corinth was given and it still applies today for proper etiquette in NEW COVENANT worship today in 1 Cor 14:26

[26] What then shall we say, brothers and sisters? When you come together, each of you has a hymn, or a word of instruction, a revelation, a tongue or an

interpretation. Everything must be done so that the church may be built up.

The requirements of New Covenant Worship are quite simple,
1. To worship the Lord in Spirit and in Truth
2. Understand that you carry the Glory of the Lord so do all to point others to Him
3. As a nation of king-priests understand that you exalt the King of Kings and Lord of Lords in your worship and not self
4. Understand that you represent the Government of God and that wonderful government is governed by Holy Spirit who will lead guide and direct your worship
5. Allow the gifts of the Spirit to flow as He gives utterance through your worship for the edification, comfort, and exhortation to the sons of God
6. Allow all things to be done decently and in order. Quite frankly if the above steps are followed then all will flow perfectly because God is not the author of confusion, He knows how to communicate with all glory carriers present.
7. Take the limits off God and off you for an UNPRECEDENTED experience, revelation, and new dimension of worship!!!!

Review Notes

Take this time to note, document, and review all that you have read and received of the Lord as you have digested this book. Walk into "THE NEW" and watch God BLOW YOUR MIND!!!!

_____
_____
_____
_____
_____
_____
_____
_____
_____
_____
_____
_____
_____
_____
_____
_____
_____

Bibliography

Book References:

Strong's Concordance **932** *basileía* (from <u>935</u> */basileús*, "king")
Webster's dictionary
The prophet's Dictionary
Zondervan's Holy Bible: KJV version, MSG Version, NIV Version, NLT Version

Other resources:

7 Hebrew postures of worship – buddysheets.tripod.com

About the Author

Doneta Dawson is a Wife, Mother, Worshiper, Author, Teacher, Singer/Songwriter, Minister and Prophet. She currently resides in Charlotte, NC and is native to Cincinnati, OH. She has been given rave reviews for Writing Ability, powerhouse vocals with range, and piercing clarity. She is known for carrying the presence of heaven through worship, teaching, and speaking to shift atmospheres and prophetically flow in song with arts ministries.

Always inspired to contribute to the world through worship and with years of experience leading worship, teaching and mentoring up and coming worship leaders, Doneta penned 'Worship Unprecedented...Kingdom Foundations in Worship'. A book that utilizes the scriptures to bring forth revelation of the Gospel of the Kingdom of God and how it shapes the worshiper's mindset as they devote time to God. Her desire is the uncover the greatest treasure hidden in plain sight and cause the worshiper to step into a new dimension to create unprecedented encounters with God.

Made in the USA
Monee, IL
30 April 2021